THE APPLE EXCHANGE

Also by S.J. Litherland

The Long Interval
(Bloodaxe Books 1986)

Four from Northern Women
(Bloodaxe Books 4-Pack 1986)

Half Light
(With Rachel Levitas, Camberwell School of Art 1988)

The Poetry of Perestroika
(Joint Editor, Iron Press 1991)

Flowers of Fever
(Iron Press 1992)

Light from a Black Hole
(Editor, Waddington Press 1997)

Free to Fly
(Editor, Richardson Press 1998)

THE APPLE EXCHANGE

S.J. Litherland

For Frances
after a marvellous reading
+ morning talk
in Durham.
love Jackie X

FLAMBARD

ACKNOWLEDGEMENTS

Some poems in this collection have previously appeared in:
Envoi, A Feather Behind My Ear, Iron, New Women Poets
(Bloodaxe Books, 1990), *Off the Shelf, Other Poetry,
Stand, Writing Women.*

S.J. Litherland wishes to thank Northern Arts for a Tyrone
Guthrie Award in 1994 to work on this book at the
Annaghmakerrig Centre in the Republic of Ireland;
also to thank Northern Arts and the Writers' Union in
St Petersburg and Moscow for financing her visit to Russia in 1991.

Many of these poems were first heard during performances
of *Earth, Water & Fire* with Margaret Wilkinson and Cynthia
Fuller on tour in Germany and in Scotland, grant-aided by the
Arts Council of England, the Kulturamt Tübingen, Durham City Arts,
the Scottish Arts Council and Clydesdale District Council.

'Death Unlimited' was written after hearing John Hartley Williams
read 'On the Island', now to be found in *Double* (Bloodaxe Books).

A section of Rachel Levitas's painting 'Waco: Fin de Siècle'
is reproduced on the front cover.

Flambard Press wishes to thank Northern Arts for its financial support.

First published in England in 1999 by Flambard Press
Stable Cottage, East Fourstones, Hexham NE47 5DX

Typeset by Harry Novak
Cover design by Gainford Design Associates
Author photograph by Barry MacSweeney
Printed by Cromwell Press, Trowbridge, Wiltshire

A CIP catalogue record for this book
is available from the British Library.

ISBN 1 873226 34 9

CONTENTS

For Rachel and Ben Levitas

'All deities reside in the human breast.'
(William Blake, *The Marriage of Heaven and Hell*)

'An agony of flame that cannot singe a sleeve.'
(W.B. Yeats, *Byzantium*)

CARNAL KNOWLEDGE

The juice of the apple ran in her veins.
Truth. Poison. The trees in the garden
lost their leaves, hymned winter. Season

went through season. Beneath the trunks
the cells ran frantic, signalling codes
of life and death. She saw the eyes of the snake

flicker like a shutter. White hairs shot
into her temples. She covered her weightier
breasts, the slight paunch of her stomach.

The apples were falling off the tree.
She couldn't run back, her mind was ahead,
stripping the garden. She had believed

in the fiction, the paradise in her
when he touched her. Euphoria
suspending drops of a waterfall and afterwards

air clearer than belief. As memory began
it was mirrored in water, truth forking across
its image, and was gone, a snake's passage

rippling the picture as time divided before
and after her. And another snake grew,
a snake of double thinking, the chevrons

on its skin pointing to North
and South as it grew, as it switched
polarities. They would coil truth and lies

together, she and her lover. The mirror
was expanding into four dimensions
and into the fifth, of imagination.

THE APPLE EXCHANGE

Paris was granted second sight.
                              In Aphrodite's
palm he saw the face of Helen and wars.
                              In Love
he saw the ten-year siege, Troy's beaches
under Greeks, the clash of passions sprung
out of the box once opened
                              the lid wrenched back
primal love, anger, hate exposed
                              energy
uncoiling from shattered stars.
                              His cool eyes
considered.
He offered the apple to Hera
                              peace triumphed
and politics smiled
                   – the world fell into order
and a shudder of opposition
                              went through
the universe.
              The fires were dying too soon
in human history.
              The price has to be paid
on the apple exchange by Paris and Eve
for our emotions, our intellect
                              to travel
to the limit of exhaustion.
                              Without propulsion
human history would collapse
                              back
into its egg.

Eve had seen the loss of innocence,
                              the bliss
of stasis,
          the unquestioning idyll

of repetitive management
                              and yawned,
the yawn had escaped her
                              echoing in paradise
and the serpent quickened in the tree
                                        the voice
of progress knew its time had come.
The universe hung in the balance
                              as she weighed
the walled garden against the wilderness.
Fruit without labour was tasteless
                              she braced herself
she would plant her own seed,
                        and the other Eve in her
held back, wanted to run back
                        to Adam and obedience
as libraries built in her mind
                        and she saw the box open,
primal thought exposed,
                        arguments arise
thought knifing thought, atrocities –
as she tried to close
                  the box and couldn't.
The universe obligingly divided to save itself:
     Eve withdrew from the tree,
                              the fruit of knowledge
     rotted,
           eternity shortened
                        to a spell of gardening.
     Eve bit the apple
                  and drew juice like blood.

Paris anguished.
                  He was between past and future,
foreknowledge and foreboding spun him on the moment.
He couldn't choose
                  and Athena was sulking
out of the contest.

The universe obligingly divided to save itself:
    Paris gave the apple to Hera
                           and the recoil began.
    Paris gave the apple to Love
                        in Aphrodite's palm
and destiny was satisfied at Love's precedent,
the prime mover with the ill train
                        fuel for the engine
the god in the machine.
                  And in the seed of the apple
the slaughter began.
               Human history could unwind and learn
of the parents of its beginning
                  and the shadow
of its sisters in its brain.

COLLAGE

Sumptuously
the lamplight
is enamelling
half my window

the cascading leaves
of the house plant
boldly printed
black on gold

In the corner
there is a silhouette
of your head
like a trademark

the tall narcissi
framed in the other half
stand elegantly
in their window box
white stars looking
outward to the dark

Whenever the past
is driven outside

my thoughts
and conversation
divide like this

arranged on one plane
from different
realities

The present is mirror/
transparent

a collage of appearances

the public and private
projected on split screens

The illusion
is the composition.

ANOTHER FLOWERING

Half wood, half flowers,
the tree struggles to follow
the masquerade of a mild

winter. Drawn upwards from
lower branches the small pink
flowers settle more each day.

Against the sleeping colours
of the hospital garden
the blossom looks unfresh,

the petals burnt out,
last year's frock dragged
out for another performance,

tinged with a grey tone.
By Christmas, if the frost
fails, the tree will host

a canopy obliterating
winter, the last base
of a thousand dying moths.

Against snow the off-colour
sprays will be exposed
as tired complexions.

Not the first flowering
still folded deep in the stem
waiting for Spring, but

another, premature or late,
ghost-flowers or pale
prototypes, flourishing

out of season; sterile moons
compared to suns, or
mothers to daughters,

orgastic flowering without
fruit, kicking up pink-grey
petticoats in the winter zone.

EURYDICE ASCENDING

You violate my dreams and leave a seed
unbolting the black. Come for me Orpheus
or if you will not come I will ascend myself
out of the darkness like a seed germinating.
We are soul-kin, your face in the mirror
looking back. Only you have the power to seduce
hell and save me, to quench fire with fire.

Our days dwindled and often we were silent
where once we talked. But our music was still
perfect pitch and we a perfect match.
Don't punish me for dying, for arguments
we couldn't transcend, spitting like cats.
You never quite believed you possessed me.
But see, see, I am like a seed ascending.

Music, Orpheus, yours and mine, is the kind
to stir the dead we think we've put aside.
Fire should drive out fire. Hell is desire,
the absence of your body inside me. In dreams
you enter and my coming is a roar in the silence.
Memories pursue him! When he is distracted
by ambition, new women, plague him Memories!

Let him be unsatisfied until he is driven
here for me. Don't release him, Soul-goddesses!
Shadow where he sleeps and wakes to some other,
only you have the power to subdue his soul.
Silence. I hear nothing. You come only in dreams.
The silence is torment where I cannot die again.
I must ascend myself, like a seed germinating.

Will I meet you face to face coming down?
And on your face will be that frown of distance
above me, when you exquisitely lay on me,
as if to say, Lady, who are you, lover
or stranger I break bread with and give
the last drop of my blood to? Will I one day
shake another in bed and sweat above her?

Or descend to hell for you, Eurydice?

THE INFORMER

You look like an informer
        the kind who shifts politics without principles.
In your informer's eyes,
in your waiter's eyes checking tables not people,
I see no memory of us.
        I'm not on the guest list of your future.
You have no feelings left. There's no error.
You travel lightly,
but in your suitcase there's a photograph
        you couldn't quite jettison – you look so good –
a young man of feeling, of passion.

IMACES

This
time round we know the game, flirting under cover,
excitement of intrusion into no man's land,
the sexuality of wooing by metaphor, the sky of desire
is fireworks without corpses. It is headier this time,
somehow more naked, exposed, but we've been here before,
so we're veterans.
Still, irresistibly I touch your hair,
almost a plaything, almost inattentively,
as if an abstract thought touched you in a caress,
and it passed by, overlooked, like a bird crossing a battlefield,
independent as a sparrow.
It flies away, becomes image,
memory, ignites a fire somewhere. Later you look helpless,
stuck to my hand and my side as you struggle to leave and cannot,
in your eyes a kind of honest greed, trapping the blue dart
of my ring in your fingers, lodestone for the moment.
What
sends you sprawling is fiction become truth, or half-truth
ready to recoil, shy once again of ending the game.

BURNING BOATS

We're having an affair
                        without being in the sheets,
we talk, talk, cross space between us often,
but we're no nearer each other.
                                You give everything
you can
        while frozen to a line,
the sword that lies in sleep; and I watch what I cannot
touch, unspoken as intimacy grows.
                                It was Lancelot
who was bound as I am, not Guinevere, who knew her knight
was hooked; only she could condescend to change the rules
and take her forbidden body to his –
did she drop a handkerchief or a straight hand
to the groin?
            Or was the first moment
lips no longer talking, eyes no longer watching but blurring,
and hands
        holding onto this moment in another life,
Fate standing there with a new garment to slip on.
All before had been guarded
                            and reversible,
                                        interchangeable
dance of friendship,
                    all now irreversible,
                                        time-chained,
sequential path of lovers.
                        It isn't only armies who burn boats
so they have to stand and fight.
                            The gesture tests us,
there on the table is the matchbox we have fiddled and played with,
emptied and filled with talk.
                    OK Guinevere,
                                strike a match.

EXILES

The hunched look of the unemployed
                              is still in your shoulders,
as you walk a little away from me –
your extra-lean cigarette become dead
in your hands
                    as your lips form a straight line;
too many days of forced living
                                   – a convict's grimness –
hardens your face, except your eyes,
they send different messages, hostages to your exile,
speak without bitterness, echo, shadow, follow
love as if watching a seagull flying out to sea
                              constantly
intimate,
            stamping and addressing postcards of desire, hope,
kindness –
            not love letters, they're not written there.

Your gypsy hair fights back too, whipping your face,
sometimes trapping your eyes,
                              frenzied black curls
which you cannot comb, left uncut to grow fallow,
not hair to get a job,
                    but will pull a lover,
sheltering my hands.

We make love
            as if this is our only meeting,
crossroads we return to.
                              You track sensation
down my leg while we're still strangers, reading
new body maps, unsettling boundaries.
We have thrown away passports and clothes,
                                   on the eve
of neither past nor future
                        possess each other.

19

You reach towards another shore of self, the one
waiting for someone.
When you wake, before it fades,

                             it is me.
I have learnt to abandon hope,

                        to cling utterly to life
and this circle of moments.

                    Nothing between us
except delicacy of new nakedness and faint smoke
from the thin cigarette you lean over for.

CONTRARIES

We reached a wakefulness
that needed punctuation.
Like a sentence without pauses
for breath.
Everything we did raised the tempo.
You tried to slow it down
but the brakes only burnt me.
I wanted to free-fall
but fell into your caution,
your resistance
which tried to pin me, trapping
me like your own trapped passion.

Somehow we were allied – you were fighting
yourself
the you stuck inside
like a genie in a bottle.
The one you'd safely corked
or so you thought,
the daemon, the demon,
the unreasonable axeman.
Everything you had been defeated by
smelt blood,
resurrection.
You accuse me like a mirror
I could shatter.
We were dividing into contraries
breeding keys and locks.

SHADOWS

You have a way with silence
                        it's a weapon of yours.
I parry it with words
                        and force you out of shadows.
Now we measure each other
                        foes of a kind,
ex-lovers carry armour.
                        Our needs clash –
you seek one road
                        the avenue of certainties,
one beloved
                        – time is your adviser
always whispering 'wait'.
                        I am sick of shadows.
I clung to your reality,
                        flesh, eyes, hair and beloved flaws.
I am tired of all or nothing.
                        I want everything in-between.
My soul ignores me
                        is plotting with your soul.
They've gone to a disco.
                        They've forgotten us.

IMPERFECTIONS

I was unsuitable
        almost from another age
                another planet
where poets gabbled in poet-speak,
              my clothes the wrong kind
of anarchy
        on the edge of clothes dialogue,
               my demands
too demanding
        as though time had no space in it
time pressed together like a cardpack
            and my needs
were hideous
        like crying babies
           the ones good mothers
come close to battering.
        And you, too,
were impossibly imperfect
        the hermit cowering in his cell
always worrying about the weather outside,
           but we made love
like visible angels
        stripping everything away to nakedness.

THE SCHIZOPHRENIC

The trees hold so many thoughts,
then let go and rest, their brain
bare and bony, skulls wintering.

The pavements are lost under
their dappling. The mosaics
fall from the trees, collect

into a single rich sensation,
hold so many thoughts as if
I absorbed the trees' annual

fall in one photograph.
Here is stasis for a second;
my brain embracing a myriad

possible forms and choosing
a star in the universe.
O the freedom and the power

before the world swirls again
dislodging the stained glass leaves
into dying fragments.

I tear my hair, bare my skull,
my thoughts struggle to fall,
my brain writhing as it petrifies.

THE DEBT PROBLEM

I must tell my story. Listen.
There will be a number of things.
Without a pause, or a metaphor,

I will relate my day. Music
will play in the background.
I hear your dutiful listening.

It doesn't matter. Inside
there is a kind of cosiness
without heat. Outside, winter.

Money is impossible. My life
is frail, my economy *Polish*
and I need substantial aid

to buy freedom. Yes this
is my lack-lustre capitalism,
two rooms I do not own.

I fantasise that I can buy
good food. Clothes are my
Christmas presents.

So many people want to sell
things to me. My debts are making
love, new younger debts will arise.

Newcastle, 1989

TRUE LOVE

A room in Moscow, the air smelling of stale sweet smoke.
A curtain hangs in gaps,
                                toilet tiles thickly set,
a frantic plumber has thumbed in joints around pipes.
Through the wall comes a Russian love song.
        But the country has fallen out of love with itself.

Yesterday it was romantically poor
                                but the lover's eyes
doubted, began to compare this botched shabby reality
with another,
                sharper, smoother, cleverer.
Something faded from the eyes of the USSR.
It struggled in tired union with itself.

Revolution is an extreme act of love
        a country in love with its future,
                metamorphosis into new beauty.
The Soviet Union looks into the mirror and sees ageing ugliness.
In abandoned Leningrad, new Petersburg, shops no longer trade,
mud silts across floors,
                        shelves display themselves.
Nevsky Prospect is full of people hiding the calamity.

A true communist is a lover in love with mankind.
        Here the love-dream is over.
                        We've been cheated,
this shabby city,
this country of romantic gesture
        sees its face in the mirror.

A true communist is a lover in love with justice.
        Here he is a failed lover, abandoning his ageing beloved.
        Now the whole world has fallen out of love with itself.
The Soviet Union, in the middle of a half-completed affair,
its belief cracked,
                        regards in horror its own entwined limbs.

Moscow, December 1991

WOLVES

I

Our driver was knowing. We were all hungry with fatalistic
readiness for something awful for lunch: a thin gruel perhaps

with fatty meat that smells. It was mid-winter Petersburg,
post-Tsar, post-Soviet, without obligation to feed guests.

It was getting dark at two without snow to lighten the streets.
The lamps, half of them missing, came on at four to save fuel.

The weather was December English: hovering around freezing
with thin slush over mud betraying municipal neglect.

Here, said our driver, with a Russian flourish, squashing the car
between others, disregard which had produced a harvest of dents.

The short street was typically grand, identical in its gestures
of elegance and symmetry, pillars and porticoes, to its neighbours.

We'd never find it again. All Petersburg was perfectly proportioned
with eighteenth-century mania for balance: metropolitan Bath

on the scale of princes. *Here* was a doorway, twice as tall as needed.
No sign, or sign of anything. The driver knocked and it opened.

We all quickly moved in – in case it might close and the unfittest
left out in the cold. Inside was a café, painted bright gloss red

with glowing red tablecloths, the type called in the war 'oilcloth' –
the war we shared with them. There was no fuss, no rush at the counter.

In the rosy light we relaxed, ordered Russian tea in glasses.
Customers were reading newspapers. We delayed hunger with curiosity.

The café had somehow survived, proletarian, still cheap
(we checked the prices). At the counter we ordered borsch and blintzes

and cakes. Cakes! Even in the hotels there were no cakes or coffee.
Our party agreed. The food was delicious. This is *good* borsch,

said our eldest with a kind of folk memory. What's the name of this
place? you asked, thinking of tomorrow's lunch. *The Fantasy Café,*

our driver replied. The next day it was still there, one last good borsch
before our night train to Moscow. I dreamt we were unravelling back

to their past, where Anna Karenina in despair threw herself under
our wheels, where weather in winter always stuck below zero, and rain

outside our window was shape-changing to snow, chasing us like wolves.

II

Midnight. It was snowing in Moscow, out in the suburbs. Plantation
rows of flats for miles. You're allowed to hijack cars. It takes

some nerve. You stand in the road and stick your hand out. This one
was revving about to go. Three of us stopped him with one thought.

It should have been a troika driven by a snow queen.
Instead we had a burly Russian male and the car we'd hailed,

commandeered as a taxi. He was affable. We'd pay for the trip.
His limousine of the Fifties cosseted us with fat ribbed seats.

He had a companion I hadn't noticed in the dark, in the snowlight
arcing around us. His companion turned round. From a ruched pocket

behind his seat he withdrew a crystal glass. It glittered like the snow
queen's crystal heart, the one so easily shattered into splinters.

His hand delved again to deliver a single bottle. A fairy story.
He was granting a wish. It was beer from the caverns of ice.

After days of wine and vodka, a gift of a god. Beer in Moscow!
Unobtainable like sugar and coffee. In the arc-lights of the snow

he let us see his face, protected by a black astrakhan collar
turned up in the manner of a prince striding into the forest

with his hawks, his coat haughty on his shoulders like a cloak.
His was an Astrakhan face from the mountains, with black glossy

curls to match the coat, his nose like a hawk's, his eyes –
those black heavy-lashed almond eyes were eyes of an icon –

eyes I'd made up in the Fifties into the doe-eyed look –
were imperious, the original form looking at mortals

whose copies would run and smudge from laughter and tears.
Beside him stirred a third from his coat, the same as his coat,

a black Astrakhan puppy, fit for a prince and his hawks.
He'd grow into a great hound, we were told, and didn't doubt it.

The prince smiled at our wide eyes. I knew he would have perfect teeth.
Was he angel or devil? Prince Lucifer amusing himself on Friday?

Bewitched, we agreed – the most beautiful man we'd ever seen.
We'd give him our judgement and the apple. Neither angel nor devil,

a conjurement of both, pagan eyes so insolent in icons,
painted again and again by artists closer to truth than doctrine,

encircled by a tightening pack of entrepreneurs selling souls.

1991

29

YOUR LANGUAGE

Here is another language, a thicker torso,
broad arms, pressing my body for affection
as well as desire, crushing my hair,

abandoning English for silence;
in your head lived your other world, sounds
of the world you were fleeing. Our language

made us mute, you were quietly laughing,
laughing like singing under your breath.
I could find no word to touch you,

then in passion you broke the truce,
unconsciously spoke in German, a word
or phrase free of distortion, more naked

than its meaning. Later, the word came again,
the first given to me in your language,
given flesh without translation.

WE ARE THIS COLOUR OR NOTHING

We are this colour or nothing, this bright gold
in your eyes or its fading. There are riches
in this autumn, fruits of our lives, not dying

but seeding, transgressing winter, love's
explosion already loose in the air. We cannot
take one seed back once spent. This is our gold,

striking its hour.
                    There's a carelessness about time,

eroding intensities, the special play of currents
spiralling. Will we drift, not pulled back, coiling
to magnetism? We will be ordinary, and nothing

will renew this colour, autumnal charge between us.
Letters arrive slowly, a meal delayed, gone cold.
What keeps us sizzling is heat, not a low fire.

PHANTOM GOLD

The worst is, I can't remember your face –
you have vanished, leaving your voice,
your phantom leather jacket, your poems

locked in their iron-wrought language
which I prise open word by word, day by day.
My new euphoria blazes here unseen,

golden in your absence. I am burning day by day,
an incendiary love, its autumn clock ticking.
I have no photograph, only words in fetters,

bonded boxes of your past. You have vanished
into a parallel world, a parallel language,
leaving behind pure sensation, not a ghost,

a metaphor stuck with leaves that burn and fall.
Is it fool's gold? Memory is starving me –
I cannot dream but my days are filled

with your language, your presence. If I doubt,
golden leaves tumble to real weather. Still,
here is this certainty absence will not stir:

for you, poet, *shade*, love floats in suspense
like gold dust clouding a liquid. An act
of juggling day by day, tested by your vanishing

which grows without a new word or your real face
dispatching all this haziness, this struggle
with language, forms, unchaining of metaphors.

UNACKNOWLEDGEMENTS

Omitted from conversation, written
out of future dialogues, I pass

into memory without a shudder of air
receiving me. My absence is unburied,

neither alive nor withered, a country
without ambassadors or consuls, off

the map of your world, as you dismember
chains link by link, letting absence

speak for all kinds of speech, a judge
never passing sentence until the parties

wander away without justice or injustice.
When it is clear my absence is conducted,

orchestrated, a concert not to be
performed, despite the stubbornly-held

belief of the audience who have written
their own programmes, everyone will leave,

unconvinced my absence has significance.

STILLNESS BETWEEN SEAS

You spot the wave to come, in sprung
seas, the wind is beginning to rise,
lull, prescient ripples form –

at this long turn, you out-face
the unsettling horizon, the first signs
of restless birds, change of season.

Stillness between seas: the words move
between tensions, prophesy an end
to this time nestling between storms,

your calm collides with new momentum
nagging like daybreak, seas let
loose to resurrect their height.

There is no compromise between day
and night, halves of each other,

dawn and dusk are changing light.

What of lives lodged between deaths?
Will we survive, the turbulence
repeating the pattern? Or never

reoccur? – chaotic as weather, evolving
like a whirlwind stirred out of calm
by a glance, drift apart like galaxies

once curled tight, born on ripples
to the brink of light where we cannot
contract to ourselves once past.

Even storms age, the universe entropies.
Time's arrow will not reverse,
changes run out of changes, the universe

tires at the edge, between the push
and pull of its seas; *this* is stillness –

before zenith hurtles back to zero.

Calmness and seas rung by each other
catch matter and space in a single ball,
or is it half of another in shadow?

Or one of many dividing moments
in time where all choices live
and in a dimension we're together?

– time memorising our lives written
like stories beginning and ending
but read at once like a drawing –

where we exit and *exist* as all
possibilities to be unravelled.
Stillness loses calm, your words imply,

the whisper of the wind rising here,
what is to come is your foreknowledge

of storms, the birds are harbingers.

ESCAPING LIGHT

You are the darkest star
                    the one imploded
to non-reflecting space
                    somewhere there
is your intensity
                    travelling inward.
Your face dispels me
                    there's no picture
in your mirror.
                    I stand here and wave
but there's no answer.
                    Only your eyes
conquer time
                    ignore our conversation
like the eyes of the astronaut
                    who has seen
the earth rise
                    still blaze
with absent certainties
                    compel me
to improvise
                    the violation of physics.

BLOOD WEDDING

that kick of authority, that rearing
we know will break into a toss of frills,

this sea wave could be the Spanish dancer
at *Blood Wedding*; the waterbreak,

patched concrete, looks impassive,
but will crumble before the sea's dashes;

there is no doubt who is the survivor –
not the watcher, but the watched.

THE FIRE FUNERAL

A Performance

Under jetting white stars, incandescent
halo masking the dark, you were defending

the dead with a firework torch, your white face
indifferent to observers, following the beat

of the drum, the waving plumes. Fireworks
fumed and cracked. You were so close I could

touch you, your black figure slight as hands
on midnight, face white as the bullfighter's

facing the bull. The funeral cart spat stars,
turning wheels slowly for martyrs, drew

applause from the crowd, shot sparks at the dark,
where the wind was waiting, its breath untempered –

blew embers under the cart. Flames curled upward
like hands trying to get out. Flames you kicked

down. The procession drummed on, dancers
leapt backwards and forwards with plumes.

I was a voice at your elbow: *It's still on fire!*
Embers cursed by sand and undone by hands

as the masque paraded driven by performance.
The pyre was lit inside white mourning screens.

You became a dark figure flitting around fuses
primed to fizz messages of ignition on wires

for the carnival funeral, the firework finale
of starlight and cracking earthbound explosions.

And the uninvited wind was forgotten.
The beast was burned and a new beast trod forth

in celebration, in procession, while flames
began to eat their cage in derision, the wind's

breath licking and stroking them, playful cubs
growing tigerish stretching their limbs,

leaping upward and biting ropes holding posts.
The fire was racing as a heart races making love,

knocking over paper doors and tumbling wires.
Danger bleeding into the air in a comet

tail of sparks while the procession dodged
falling masts and the crowd was pitched in –

enthralled by drama and life locked in a battle
of control, neither gaining the mastery,

a struggle of pride, of nerve, of judgement,
when to cut and run, when to march and play on.

NOTES ON A SEASON IN HELL

Hell is beautiful. My soul knows this, is appalled.
A place where no promise is kept. On offer

is everything flowering, emotions unstemmed, a bleeding
of time, of purpose. Hope survives here forever,

its tendrils push out of the grave, condemned
to creep upwards. The resurrection is eternal.

My soul is invisible. Everyone is reading
the book of their ego. Hell is full of conversation

but no-one is listening. Everyone is writing a book
of their ego, letters full of news no other is reading.

Monologues are exchanged, fires that do not fuse.
Everywhere there are mirrors that do not reflect me.

Only eyes skim the surface, skid on the surface
like landing birds, pause to enquire, fly off.

My body is haunting my soul, hungry to talk, touch,
love, locked out from communication.

Everyone desires me, their eyes watch from a distance,
restless trapped eyes, eyes switched on, loaded.

They are swimmers in a dry pool. It will never happen.
Only in fantasies will they frolic, consume their fire.

DISSENTING ANGEL

To Epstein's 'Lucifer 1945'

That sensual face gives birth
to instinct, your angelic form
already too human, full
of appetite for life, nascent

fall – surrendering into time
and all the colours of light.

Your hands, delicate as shells,
repress the thought, conjured

out of the tiniest seed
of obstinacy – it will explode
into rebellion, your weight
poised forward, your beauty meant

for touching, the golden rapture
you expose alighting on the edge
of all experience. Are we made
in your image? The perfect

imperfect form we shadow,
spirit and flesh in perpetual
strife – you see it all, the crazy
plunge from submission, the spurning

of peace become narcotic –
the shift in balance, the tilt forward,

is motion you drag with hands
pressed out in apprehension.

What did you do? Refuse to worship?
Turn anarchist, republican?

Pride, the greatest sin, you
wore a cockade in your cap –
because of you we won't wait

for heaven to settle scores,
rebellion-fostered, souls-ignited.

Patron saint of levellers,
the first to throw dust in the eyes
of mastery, in a gesture of disgust

and scorn, release from their box
the first questions and first arguments
bouncing out like curls,

like endless paradigms of chaos
a triple mirror of eternal images,
from your vain curiosity –

the need to find your own face,

patron saint of arts and sciences,
and discontented humanity
saying *no*, the divine word of dissent,

called, by those who want order, evil
but there's no evil in your face

only hesitation and desire
to flex the muscles you've been given.

Promethean, bearing punishment
so we can have the gift of fire,
you tempted Eve to see innocence

as ignorance, paradise as locks
on her mouth, showed her the apple
in the branches where you and God

fought and gave it fruit.

If God is gravity, you're explosion,
bursting from his singularity,

his moment of timelessness.

Lucifer, you learned to love yourself
and were damned to discover loneliness.

God couldn't break your spirit.
Don't repent! You and he are one,

split into two, invented equality.
We sense right and wrong

in mysterious measure
of the weight in each hand.

If there's harm in the world,
the cruel games we play

come from hierarchy, playing God
with torture and torment

on those who won't serve us.
You didn't invent Hell – *he* did.

Prime spirits, essences:
he, the Law, you subversive.

Milton knew democracy was born
with you, and couldn't square

his circle of autocrat and rebel.
Paradise well lost he might

persuade us against his will –
he came to love you, Lucifer,

the first free spirit – the sinner
God loves the most, the one

he's obsessed with: his beloved.
Excess of love drives him

to regain you, to recapture you,
cage you in omnipotence,

and Revenge chases you
around all spaces, and bitterness

would lash you to nothingness
if it could, but you're immune,

once free, to coercion.
The equation is: tyrants breed

usurpers. Rebels are made, Lucifer,
like us, not born – and we're

not survivors, but fighters.
We have to be careful we don't

bully in turn, in our arrogance
not see the switch in power,

rebels in clothes of emperors
demanding new obedience.

I can't pray to you but we can talk.
Lucifer, I need a lover,
someone to speak to my body

in her language, to let her speak.
She's in a land of strangers,
there are eyes at the windows,

watching, but the doors are shut.
She has a key in her soul.
If it fits they change the locks.

She's in hell, Lucifer,
your territory, where her flames
are invisible and can't die.

No-one pities her, but pity
isn't your department. She pities
herself, untouched.

Ripe apples about to wither
uneaten might feel a sense of waste
if they could, feel time

shifting the balance from ripeness
to rot and she's helpless
as the months start dropping from

the tree, and there's no-one
to heal her dumbness.
She's a pariah. I've sold her

to you. She'll forego love
for freedom, independence,
equality, if that's the price

exacted by lovers at the door.

Let me admit, Lucifer,
I understand God's point of view,
our hands empty of holding our lover
no power on earth, heaven or hell

can win back, no enticement.
He's nurturing grievances,
driven by an insult we overlooked,
my own Lucifer turning to hiss

at my caress, where once he stood
he's gone. Like God I've learned
there's nothing worth having
that's not given in free will –

though he's all possession
wrung by your independence:
you'll fight eternally, you two.
    He's stronger but you're fiercer.

He'll wait until you tire
and when your indignation
is tightened within his grip
to the tiniest seed of fire,

he'll pursue you with his power
down the narrowest corridors
where time's crushed out of existence,
and you'll turn when cornered,

fed by resistance, to face him
with tenderness, your hands raised
in distress, to restrain his final
assault before you explode.

Captive, you clawed yourself free –
God challenger – you *are* energy,
breaking out of control
closing down infinitely

without you. Your fate to swing
the pendulum, ring changes,
to start history. Your bequest
is fearlessness as you look

into your descent and pause,
    and say *to hell with it*, curve
your soul into a somersault –
light the morning sky like a fuse.

EXIT LINES

At the end of the meal
                           the banquet of wounding
the feast of broken mirrors
                           we were offered
sweets
          one white one red.
                           Which one
do you want? you said.
                           I chose the red,
dark as blood, a ripe raspberry, full of juice.
I thought you would, you said
                           with bitterness.
Why, which one do *you* want?
                           I offered, confused,
not touching the sweet.
                           The white, you said,
and we ate our choices.

SHELLEY AT SIXTY

You survived the storm,
                    survivor's eyes defend a narrowing life,
perspective lines nearing their natural point of oblivion.
There's jauntiness of the ex-sailor
                    you twirl a hand, energy
leaps upward from disturbed coals, then settles again.

Women rouse you, your eyes collect them. You can still take
one or two – without asking too much,
                    and if you've fattened, so what?
You're a tougher goat not a unicorn,
                    there's wisdom in thicker haunches
and tenderness outlasting love.

In you fire and water fight on, the water's gaining as you face
the second threat of drowning.
                    The first time you hung on, defying
Providence and romance.
                    This time you need to let go,
but you can't, your fists still tight around the spar
although the storm died thirty years ago
                    and the water
is only a foot deep you'll soon lie in.

You plot to outwit the stars,
                    fence your life against gypsies,
nurse the spark
                    in the dark fire instead of putting more fuel on,
bed the muse not too often,
                    out of one piece of perfection
make a single garment.

Your anger's turned to spite, your despair to coldness,
your rage to temper.
                    It's a way of keeping reserves.

You think of exhausted mines
                              and practise moderation.
It's a poet's fault to think by metaphors –
                              no phoenix
on your horizon,
the east wind supplanting the west
is cooling your ashes, redrafting your words.

LE GENTILHOMME SANS MERCI

You sprang on my doorstep with your changeling face
and shy, defensive gestures as if shutting
and opening secret gates. *This was partly true.*

You entered like a salesman or customer appraising
property, your eyes noticing age. But you liked
my house, tension uncoiling from you, a snake

you might hang up with your coat. Still, your eyes
betrayed your otherness, calculating
and flitting over my face, edgy looks of a bird

approaching a bird-bath set out by humans.
A fumbler, yet poised, an actor playing a clown
who played the part of prince the other night.

As lover you were a surprise, the third attempt
you found our form, banished the confines
of a shabby flat, took us to reedbanks, parting

the grasses of my hair to kiss me, laid me on air
before lowering me to earth in perfect landing,
lapping us with leaking waters. Too soon

I remembered tales of cold enchantment,
your puckish face impatient for me to leave
your world, irritated by my mortality, suffering

a moment of tenderness – to be uprooted as a weed
of human love already rooted. *This was partly true.*
The customer reconsidered, switched brightness for a cloak.

CONVERSING WITH STATUES

your hands follow in your mind
        their flesh in stone
would cup the breast your words
        so delicately hold

        as your eyes convert the stone
the honing of your language
as it hovers in air above statues

this is a kind of ecstasy and yet
the air is distance, holding
        your language waves

adroitly you have dropped
        into my mind, my soul,
the teasing inkdrop of your sensuality
        your penstrokes deep as claws

we're not just connoisseurs
        we're the clay, the stone

DEATH UNLIMITED

Have I got it right? I saw your words so clearly.
Not as language, as presence. He was making love
to someone, somewhere in the street. A corner?
It might have been fucking. It doesn't matter.

What shattered, transfixed me was your indirect
image. The ravens flying overhead turned to crystal.
Was that right? Or have Chinese whispers changed birds
into crows? I saw them – the ravens – flying in a kind

of formation, suddenly frozen by his orgasm.
Their flight stopped by time suddenly stopping,
crystallised by shock. And, presumably,
afterwards, they started flying again, as the lovers

unclenched, got back into knickers and trousers.
For me, they're stuck there, those crystal birds.
They can't move on, blasted by ecstasy into something
captive like ice, which won't melt, like trauma.

Some would say: Disband them, change the image.
We're poets, illusionists, get out the projector –
wind back the reel to where the birds are trapped,
and back, free the ravens. Desire is reversible.

We're not in the restaurant where we ate the meal
and the bill we won't pay lies on the table
in a future we've walked out on. Any other problems?
We can reorder the universe, shrink the big bang,

invent God and imagine life after death as negative
energy, where the things we didn't do or failed
to complete turn up, all that footage we cut out
or merely contemplated, death has time for.

Death is where images we never used are stored,
the novels we never wrote, where there's plenty of room
for unspent desire. In life that's all curtailed.
In life we have to choose, the moment is the axis

of past and present, and at every step the axis moves.
And what's happened to the crystal birds? The image
is preserved. The lovers are still at the corner
of the street. The ravens are flying overhead

and at the moment of orgasm time suddenly stops,
sets the scene like the motif on a Willow Pattern plate.
We live by the shock of what we think we remember,
bequeath everything we've forgotten to death.

GETHSEMANE

Night air is scouring the garden, there's hardly
any colour, a blur of heavy green and charcoal,
rocks magnetise what's left of moonlight. Dawn

is not yet here, the ordinary dawn unaware
of prescience in several minds. The garden breathes
its presence stirring trees and skin of cold sand.

Time is lulled but not asleep. Eyes are fireflies
flitting anxiously in dark foliage. At this moment
choices abound in all minds but one, yet paths

are converging on his path. The garden is a womb
in one sense, in another a tomb. The dawn is lit
below the horizon, inevitability a relief

of order, backcloth to our uncertainties:
the soldiers unseen until they appear, except
by one holding all strategies of conduct, who

allows play to go on. All but he moves blindly
into the future, the path of a footstep leading
into a storm of colliding moments, chaos tossing

intentions on a sea or spilling them apart like drops.
He, with glasses of foresight perched on his nose,
sees by infra-red through the darkness, sees

the mind of Judas as he approaches, the shallows
flowing over the disturbances of his soul, the soul
that will be flayed. As god reaches for godhead

he's accepting sacrifices. The expectations
of time are to be desecrated, not time residing
in the roots of trees, the atomising of sand,

but time born of time where the snowflake's
fall cannot be guessed, unwoven until interaction.
The dawn's welcome for its everyday appearance,

colours are running back into trees, rocks, sand,
highlighting faces, eyes. Judas treacherously
kisses the man he loves, not the first to do so

or the last. His instinct for survival prompts him:
his birthright, denying the subterranean level
of his soul moving in the opposite direction

like the wind against a storm. The kiss is planted
like a cross to mark the spot, frailty gathered
in the arms of a god who has the power to spare him

but will not. In the mind of the god paths are held
like reins. He neither urges nor stops them. He's not
that blind mortal thing. He's not discarded his inner

sleepless eye, letting Judas blunder into remorse,
offering him choices from a marked deck of cards.
He's here waiting for injury like a wronged wife.

Already there's reproach in the kiss he returns,
that animal pledge of trust, that fearful loving
touch of lips on lips as sun kisses the tops of trees.

A STORY ABOUT CRICKET

I'm sure Hera looked down from Olympus
and spotted someone like you. (I'm sure
she did.) Bored with your work, herding

a few goats and sheep, taking time out
to play the lyre and sing. And she came
down to offer celestial conversation,

watching as you talked: your slim build,
bare arms, still hands, one wrist braceleted
with a woven rainbow thread, the single

ring on your finger; discovered your humour
defending yourself with deft strokes
flourished like a Gower of those times,

before the game was shaped from mood
and movement; you, displaying fair curls
like his as you talk, curls she hadn't

noticed until you touched them, your fair
beard hiding your youth, blue eyes hiding
your intensity most of the time.

Hera couldn't force you like Zeus
or seduce you like Aphrodite,
dreamt instead of her immortal soul

snaking into yours as you conversed.
That's what she dreamt. I know she did.
Powerless to touch you or your mind,

the man behind the mind, desiring the soul
inside the man where you are both equal.
This is a most conventional story.

Actually, you spotted her unaware,
noticed her inability to see you,
her naked face innocent of coquetry.

Hera caught in a moment of neglect.
You were the one watching who threw
a question, eyes sharp with attention

she suddenly saw and faltered at.
The Fates had delivered to her door
a beautiful young man. She couldn't

believe her luck except he was mortal.
Hera talked to her not-yet-cricketing
shepherd, dreamt of desire like a snake-

clasp coupling, desire where poetry
and music meet and hold fast, where
seamlessly we change into each other

leaving ourselves on the outside like clothes.
But don't think I'm Hera. This is only
a story about the beginning of cricket.

How it started as an art of conversation,
a wish of seduction, a compromise
of attraction, a sport they think

began among shepherds by a wicket gate
without the intervention of the goddess.
After five days Hera devised a game

in your image, of courtly strategy
and attack, tactics and defence,
above all, of fair play and deference

to a question of judgement, where
her soul and yours are the players
held together and apart by the rules.

A SONG AND DANCE

You make the atoms in my bones dance in their spaces.

I shake, judder, like an express train. Believe me

the atoms in my bones are dancing in their spaces.

My heart is an insect with a tiny life drumming
its fast metabolic rate in my ear. We couldn't
make love. I would miss you by several lifetimes.
I'm just too quick for courtship lasting centuries.

I'm broken down to atoms dancing in my bones by the look

in your eyes. It might as well be light from the stars.
This is longing unfixed as an explosion, tearing
through words like fire, breaking everything down
to shaking ash. We have to start from this collapse,

inorganic lives without language – stones, rivers,
coalescing before language creeps over like foliage.
We carry these atoms like memories and when we meet

the atoms in my bones dance and sing in their spaces,

uncrowded by deliberation of slower things.

WHAT DIDN'T HAPPEN IN THE FOYER
OF THE ARMSTRONG JAMES BUILDING

You didn't come swinging through glass doors,
the you that at every moment would
materialise from the empty morning,

your hair sweating from rain, and from
your eyes the first, unprotected, glance –
the appraisal of recognition before

ease of manners shut it down, not out of
that sterile light remaining uncrossed
by your swift stride like a too still

reflection that would not admit you.
You didn't interrupt the surface tension
of the foyer where two sat facing.

One surrendered to smoke in the drizzle,
the other shifted seats and circled.
I never moved, noticed or unnoticed

by exiting strangers, waiting too long
for an entrance that never happened, a ghost
you claimed to have missed as I missed you,

simultaneously blinded by a rogue moment
from another hour or a hole in the bag
of excuses you reached for, practising your voice

to the pitch of indignation: *Where were you?*

THE SINGING LESSON

waking from another goodbye: you fenced off by a coat collar
as we pared down months to minutes, to the no-nonsense of 3 a.m.

car conversation, almost like completing a sale; I signing
my name on the dotted line of necessity with a certain dignity;

waking after hours of numb night to find snow had written its elegy
on the morning, as if winter had given ear to my unacknowledged

pain, run through its repertoire to lay aside November rain,
wrapping my wounds in attentive bandages in a solemn hospital bed

where the weather was my visitor bringing me these flowers; sung
its elegy over the memory of your displeasure, ignoring me in

company like an unfavoured child because I'd stepped on your pride,
daring to question your right to dispose of your time as you wished;

for this I was to be crucified on the cross of the hours, and for
good measure you'd sing in your square of world like an angel

love songs for my ears while I was shunned, leaning over to another,
with a shower of fading sparks striking the air towards her –

while the void between us was dark and cold; I who dared to ask
why, for this I was to be slapped down by love on display, the love

I can't have and must be punished for: you stroking your music,
the flare of your fingers over strings ending with a movement of

smoke spiralling from a candle put out; over this the snow had blown
in the short night like the descent of pity, the word *enough* falling

PHOENIX FIRE

It's something the soul is aghast at:
the resurrection of the body in flames.

A last glow, a wink in the cold of the desert
night where the bird has gone to germinate:

it wants to keep vigil on memories. The moon
intense as the sun we can't look at: its mirror.

The moon a dead globe shining on the thing
that can't die, that's dying and regenerating,

broken down to ash where atoms are busy falling
in love with atoms, even broken down to dark

space where light still appears like bubbles.
The phoenix has no choice of suicide.

It's on the other side, forgetting its previous
span, wound through a black hole, each time

a new experience, everything chanced afresh.
The universe might die overburdened with detail,

but not yet, the phoenix won't forever light itself,
but not yet, I won't fall in love again, *but not yet*.

OSCAR

Style was holding me together, bridges over gaps, holes
springing in my fabric. Don't ever mock style! Take it away

and many of us would disappear, shrunk into the reversal
of our aplomb, all that posturing you want to puncture.

Ask the schizophrenic offered a cup of cheap tea
and biscuits how his esteem feels. When what he wants

is my best blue china to live up to. There's a buried dandy
in any tramp. It's the spectrum, you see. If we can't be red,

we'll be blue. Can't you smell the style in absolute despair,
in sleeping out? What might rescue us isn't kindness, but

recognition of pride in a world of paper cups, to make us
feel we're not disposable. What might save the world next

time is the soul of socialism with my kind of flair.
Others had their go, those committees of exchange

and distribution, and mostly they were fair or tried
to be – when they weren't slipping something to themselves.

At best they managed a state canteen when what we wanted
were *cafés*. The cell they broke me in was absence of style,

invisible lack of everything to nurture me. I'm like that.
The puritan who survives thinks he has the answer. Rigour

for him or her is the cure. For me, it's death in the tower
on the concrete estate where the poet is confined.

And when they put me in the press and squeeze,
and the champagne in the blood runs out, I'll be just

a shadow, a wreck you'll avoid, a street passenger,
one of the eyesores you're ignoring at your peril. My kind

want glamour, and will take it with a stolen car, not stolen
for sale but for thrills. They won't die with Oscar

on their lips, but I know their need better than you do:
dispensers of the bare minimum to the down and out.

I have my friends, Morris and Co, and the long-nosed Cyrano,
purveyors of Style. Watch those waistcoats, they're creeping in!

Watch out for the earring, it's about! The bracelet hung
on his wrist! And those boots he'll pull on to strut in!

The best thing we ever did was to make our flag red.
Such a pretty colour, the colour of happiness and blood,

a flag of passions. We never did live up to it. Not a portion
of the infinite. What everyone had was prison-cloth grey.

And when you read this, it'll be my epitaph, written the way
my pride dictates when I'm down to my last flattering kiss.

PARTY FOR A WARTIME CHILD

Watching you sing the whole of me goes silent
as you ease off your waistcoat in preparation

for hanging your guitar, strapped over your graceful
back and shoulders, held at arm's length, cradled

in fingers that have a language of mute signs
and elegant flourishes, drawing off a phrase

with a whisper uncoiling into air or pulse
with the fast rocking of your hips shivering

time to the heartbeat of a lover close to climax.
Tension in the angry flip of your hair, jerked

out of your eyes as a cloud of curls, rattled
like a bag of sweets Love offers that can't be tasted.

You're sweating in your flowered party shirt,
ripples snaking from the nexus of your hips –

body, voice, guitar, song, all moving in a stream
quivered by heat, you are the movement's child,

involuntary as a shudder. Hungry for relief
you immerse in fire as you perform the lawlessness

of passion without its crisis. You've given yourself
where yes and no co-exist, where my desire, quiet

as a wartime child at a party we only had by talk,
is offered the smell of sweetness so close to taste,

watching the singing language of your body always silent.
In the spotlight an earring flashes its undercover

warning and in lonely space above your wrist
a dark bracelet orbits its sly ring of attraction.